Exceeding Abundantly

Do You Know Who You Are?

Dorothy Muthoka - Kagwaini

PARTRIDGE

A Penguin Random House Company

To order additional copies of this book, contact
Toll Free 800 101 2657 (Singapore)
Toll Free 1 800 81 7340 (Malaysia)
orders.singapore@partridgepublishing.com

www.partridgepublishing.com/singapore

Bible Citations

Revelation12:11

Exodus17: *14*

Jeremiah3:15

1st Kings 2: 23-24

John15: 16

2nd Peter1:4

Philippians 2: 27

Genesis 15:6

Hebrews3: 13

2nd Timothy3:14-15

Hebrews5:14

Hebrews13:16

Deuteronomy28

Isaiah48:17

Psalms143:8

Ecclesiastes 9:11

Isaiah 61: 7

Matthew 6:33

John 6:28-29

Philippians 2:14

Exodus 15: 21-27

Psalms 109:1-4

Genesis 30:2

1ˢᵗ Peter1:4

Psalms 34:6

Psalms12: 2-3

Romans 13:8

Philippians 3:19-21

Numbers21:5

Judges 6:14-16

Psalms 34:9

Luke16:12

Isaiah43:19

Ephesians 1:17

1st Corinthians 15

Hebrews 8:11-12

Ecclesiastes 11:1

Job1:4-5

Hebrews 9 and 10

Ezra 7: 18-20

John15:16

John16:23-26

Job19:25-26

1 John 5:14-15

Psalm 91

2 Corinthians 5:7-10

Ephesians 3: 19-20

Psalms 90: 9

Romans13:11-14)

Revelation 5:10

Psalms, 115: 1-2

Psalms 113

Hebrews 19:19

Contents

DEDICATION

To come this far, has taken so many people who have impacted me positively but above all, my dedication is to my heavenly Father for without Him I can't and would not have done anything. My dear parents (Mr. and Mrs. Simon B.M.Muthoka) who made me realize the love of God over my life. Despite the happenings of life, God's unconditional love does not change.

To my sweet husband (William K. Mwangi) who never gave up on me even when life was so difficult. He believed in me and encouraged me to go for my dreams that were overwhelming. To my lovely children (Christine Baraka and Matthew Amani) thank you.

To my brothers (Peter Muthoka and Paul Muthoka) who always stuck with me no matter what. You always prayed for me and shared any word of knowledge over my life. To my sisters (Margaret Muthoka-Kimweli and Flora Mwende-Munyao) we grew together loving each other and protecting each other.

To Sarah Akelola and my students, you gave me the reason to fight harder and see the bigger picture that God was unveiling over my life. To my colleagues, thank you.

To all my readers, thank you for taking this opportunity to read this book. May it be a life changing experience as we learn together! It will be a life changing especially the way you view God.

FOREWORD

This book is an autobiography of Dorothy Muthoka—Kagwaini. Dorothy narrates her life story which has very important lessons for. From her young life, she touches on critical issues of family, sickness, studies, job, career and even death. These are issues that are not unique to Dorothy. Dorothy poses several questions including, one on identity, where to turn when difficult and challenging situations arise.

She also poses the question of who we attribute our success to. Throughout the book, Dorothy paints a positive attitude of hope without which life would meaningless. In this book, Dorothy, shares her life experiences pointing to one who does not change, "The God of the Bible".

I have known Dorothy to be a Godly, motivated, positive, and a hardworking lady. She has managed to strike a balance between her professional development and her devotion to God and family. She is a great inspiration to young people who are often getting caught up in the pursuit of success at the expense of family and Godly character.

This book has really inspired me and I highly recommend it. I know it will have a positive impact over your life. Try it!

Dr. Abraham K. Waithima,

Department of Economics, Daystar University.

ACKNOWLEDGEMENT

I must first acknowledge my God, who is the orchestrator of this whole idea since last year August, 2013. He told me that he has done so much with my life and I need to testify of His goodness. For the Bile says in Revelation12:11 *"And they overcame him by the blood of the Lamb and by the word of their testimony; and they loved not their lives unto death"* (KJV). I was a little hesitant as I wondered if I had heard well. To confirm His words, the following morning when I was reading my Bible, He led me to the life of Moses after the children of Israelites had defeated the Amalek. God told Moses in Exodus17: *14 "And the Lord said Moses, write this for a memorial in a book, and rehearse it in the ears of Joshua: for I will utterly put*

out the remembrance of Amalek from under heaven" (KJV). Isn't God real and good?

Since the start of the year 2013, God gave me an opportunity to hear His word through Bishop TD Jakes in the message, *"Your answer is blowing in the wind"*. He challenged us that "we must survive the test of being forgotten and rejected to be recognized. So that when you are recognized you survive the test of being noticed. This is because what you think is attacking you is really training." That was really amazing. In addition, my Pastor Lee Woo Cheol of Yuljeon Church challenged us "if you are a child of God and believe in Him, you should be controlling the world and not be controlled by the world". Finally, Pastor Joseph Prince daily devotional messages were coinciding with exact same words God was teaching me throughout the year. Then I understood the word in Jeremiah3:15 *"And I will give you pastors according to mine heart which shall feed you with knowledge and understanding"* (KJV).

To my mentor Mrs. Grace Kabuye, who always believed in me, even when I made mistakes in life . . . You have always guided me and wished me success in life. To my former Vice Chancellor in Daystar University, Prof. Godffrey Nguru; thank you for your guidance in my career; I wouldn't be where I am without your direction. To Prof. Samuel Katia thank you for allowing God to use you in my life.

To all my friends, Daystar University Community, and Yuljeon Church family; May God always shower them with his blessings.

CHAPTER 1

The Journey Begins

Whatever the mind of man can conceive and believe, it can achieve

Napoleon Hill

Welcome to my humble family background. I am the third born girl in a family of five children. My parents worked as civil servants in Kenya; my mother was a Primary School teacher and my father was a Probation Officer. We lived in many parts of the country as my parents were posted to various working regions by the Government. Kenya has over forty two different native languages. I never learned my native language which is Kamba until I was mature enough. This is because we lived in Kiambu District; a different area from my home District where the predominant language is Kikuyu. Ha! This was God's way of preparing me for a Kikuyu husband years later . . . I learned reading and writing Kikuyu language in addition to Swahili and English. My parents did everything in their power to make sure we got sound education and basic needs. This was not an easy endeavor as their income was quite meagre. As you know growing up in Africa money is really a scarce resource.

I remember a time when we were growing up; shoes were a big deal as well as having a school uniform that did not have patches all over. My parents made sure that all the school tuition fees and toiletries were paid. This left us with not enough pocket money as we would have wished for. Instead of appreciating what our parents did for us and sacrificed their comfort for us, we always complained and grumbled. One time I had been expelled out of school due to lack of school fees. Arriving home, it was so sad to see my parents in abject poverty that a daily meal and basic necessities were hard to come by. How selfish was I? My parents could hardly afford a decent meal so that we can get school fees and other needs. Maize and beans were their staple food, not to mention unaccompanied porridge. That was the day I got to understand that my parents loved us more than themselves.

When all this was happening, my mum had been diagnosed with arthritis. In the beginning, we did not know what this disease was all about. Suddenly, mum could not cook for us, wash us, nor even take care of us as she used to. This was a terrible blow to us. She was in so much pain that she could no longer cry but groan. During that time, I was in primary school in class three. We would all go and kneel besides our mum's bed not to pray but just to cry with her. When I could not take it any longer, I ran to the store and hid myself there and not talk to anyone. I preferred solitude. Family roles shifted. Dad had to take mum's role of cooking, shopping groceries and anything we literally needed. Dad you are a gem. This went on but not for so long, because we had to mature faster than our age. We had to be responsible, and learn to love each other dearly. However, we learned to share house chores and responsibilities; from the youngest to the eldest. No cheating! If one did not do their house chores, it meant no food. So we diligently did our work without fail. Up to today, when we all meet for family gatherings, everybody just knows what to do without being told. We always used to go places together, do things together and fight for one another whenever one of us got into problems with other kids. In fact, one neighbor confessed to me that she thought me and my brother were girlfriend and boyfriend because we always walked together every time, and everywhere.

We had to learn to massage mum's legs and hands with hot water as she was not able to touch cold water at all. Within a few months mum's hands and legs started changing and then got deformed. I did not comprehend or understand what was happening. Since mum was a primary school teacher, children at school would cajole and laugh at her. I imagine this was not easy but she learned to overcome it. At one time I must confess that I was also ashamed of my mother . . . I wanted her to be like "other normal mums". I wanted her to come and visit me in school; I wanted her to be beautiful with no deformation; I wanted her to put on normal shoes; I wanted people not to take notice of her disability and appreciate her as she is . . . I wanted . . . I wanted . . . the list went on. Sometimes I would even ask her; "mum does God really love you? Then why does He not heal you and you faithfully go to church?" She replied and said, "God allows circumstances to come over our lives for a reason and a purpose. You remember it happened to Job in the Bible!" I was not convinced then. I just agreed with her for the sake of agreeing.

However, the most beautiful thing that my mum did during that time was to teach us Bible stories which were so interesting to identify with. Oh! I loved those times. It made me forget that mum was undergoing any problem. Consequently, to us she taught us never to laugh or mock somebody who had a physical disability. I remember the story she shared in 1ˢᵗ Kings 2: 23-24 *"And he (Elisha the prophet) went up from thence unto bethel: and as he was going up by the way, there came forth little children out of the city, and mocked him, and said unto him, Go up, thou bald head; go up thou bald head. And he turned back, and looked on them, and cursed them in the Name of the Lord. And there came forth two she bears out of the wood, and tare forty and two children of them"* (KJV). That put fear in us that up to today when I am in the midst of people who look down on others or speak evil against others I tell them that is not good . . . if they still cannot hear . . . I disappear immediately from their presence as I know the repercussions. Anyway, I know how it feels. Been there!

When I joined High School, to me it was a turnaround of my life. I knew God, I knew Jesus Christ but it was until then that I had a transformation of my life. I accepted Jesus as my savior. I was not afraid to say that I was born again. I learned how to pray for myself, I learned to test God on His word and that was the most important thing in my life even till today. I remember this so vividly like it was yesterday, I told God that mum would never die until I said so . . . I believed this words so much . . . that one day mum called us together and she told us . . ."If I die now, you only have yourselves to take care of each other". I think, she felt she was coming to the end of herself. I went to my hiding place and reminded God what I had asked him that mum will never die until I said so. I reminded God John15: 16 *"Ye have not chosen me (God), but I have chosen you, and ordained you, that ye should go and bring forth fruit, and that your fruit should remain: and that whosoever ye shall ask of the Father in my name, he may give it to you"* (KJV).

Currently, it is now thirty years ago and mum is still alive and strong. Being with mum all my life, I have seen her fight fear, disappointment, sympathy and pity. She worked until the last day of her retirement with all the support from dad. I am now convinced that God loves mum and us. He can never allow any temptation to come our way that we are not able to bear. God never gives a load that we have no ability to bear. Mum always confessed that God loves her and will one day make her whole. I understand that God has given mum to us the way she is, as a gift. She does not have to depend on us as it was in the early years. She is independent and no longer in pain despite the physical deformation. By and by I have stopped seeing her physical disability and started having a thankful heart of appreciating God and the fact that mum is alive. Wow! I am so proud of her. Nowadays, due to mum's perseverance spirit I believe that one day, she will be made whole. This is because God's promises are precious and great so that by them we may be partakers of divine nature, escaping corruption that is in the world through lust. Like Paul I can say: For indeed mum was sick nigh unto death, but God had mercy on her and not on her alone, but on me also, lest I should have sorrow upon sorrow (2nd Peter1:4 and Philippians 2: 27). The word that says by his stripes we were healed always it is in the past tense. Look! The word is "healed" It is in past tense, not present, or future present tense. So I believe totally that I will stand and testify the goodness of the Lord in my mum's body. Anyway, if it took Abraham to receive his promise when he was a hundred years ago, then, it shall still come to pass for mum. Abraham believed God and it was accounted to him as righteous (Genesis 15:6).

High school for me went rather fast. Upon completion, to my disappointment, I had not achieved the grade that I wanted all along. I couldn't be admitted to any of the public universities. And my parents would not have afforded a private university. It was so devastating for me to see all my dreams being shuttered.

My two siblings were all in high school while my older brother and sister had gotten scholarships to go and study abroad. I was the only one left in the house. To my parents, they had done their best. However; I was feeling like a "black sheep in the family" because my life had stopped suddenly and nothing made sense. However, I kept confessing that one day I will join university even if I will have to pay for myself.

During that time I noticed every morning before breakfast, dad read the Bible continuously, while mum would go for prayer time with her fellow women prayer partners in the evening. Mum knew in this world you can never leave alone. In Christianity, we all need each other as long as it is called today, that we may exhort each other lest any of us be hardened through deceitfulness of sin. (Hebrews3: 13). I got to know a daughter of one of my mum's prayer partner who was experiencing the same challenge I was going through. We both got together and started attending lunch time fellowships. Wow! We had fun together, as we were being taught basic Bible doctrines in the fellowship. Actually, that is where I learned about tithing, offerings, giving God my time and praising from the bottom of my heart. Thank to my Pastors and Bishop. 2nd Timothy3:14-15 encourages us *"But to continue in the things which thou hast learned and hast been assured of, knowing of whom thou hast learned them; and that from a child thou hast known the holy scriptures, which are able to make thee wise unto salvation through faith which is in Christ Jesus"* KJV. After, some few months my friend joined a Technical College and again I was left at home alone. I would ask God questions like: {Lord, have you forgotten me? Why are all these happening to me? You say you have a good plan for me . . . where is it?}It took more than one year at home just hoping for an opportunity to join college. My dad got a Teachers' Training College for me to go and become a teacher but I declined. That was not my career idea. I wanted to become an Accountant. So, I told my dad, I did not want to become a teacher as everybody in the family as well as my extended family's members were all teachers. I wanted something different. It was difficult for my dad to understand what I was talking about. But he gave me an ear and he never pushed his wish on me. However, that meant extending another one year in the house as dad tried getting an alternative for me. I imagine he was disappointed in me but he chose to give me a chance.

I perfected the art of doing house chores in the house. I would iron dad's shirt perfectly, polish his shoes and made sure food was ready on time. I had no choice as all my friends were busy in college and universities. Later, I got an admission letter to go and study an Accounting course in a Training School but, I could only start from the lowest level due to my low high school grades.

Lesson learned from my heavenly Father:

❖ Children need to appreciate their parents and recognize that parents do everything in their power to make their livelihood comfortable.

❖ We must learn to listen and hear God in every area of life. This requires reading the word of God to know His will. Also, to exercise our senses so as to discern both good and evil (Hebrews5:14).

❖ We must learn to appreciate whatever God brings our way or whosoever God brings our way. Many times we do not know what we have until it has gone.

❖ The adage is true: what we confess we actually possess . . . confess success and you will be successful.

❖ Keep your conversations pure as the Bible says *but to do good and to communicate forget not: for with such sacrifices God is well pleased* (Hebrews13:16) KJV.

CHAPTER 2

A Cry for a Job

You can never cross the ocean until you have

the courage to lose sight of the shore

Christopher Columbus

I was privileged to get a casual job in an accounting office in one particular organization. That meant if there was a public holiday, I would not receive my wages on that day. The term 'casual' kept haunting me. However, for me, I loved my job because it was a source of income and it enabled me to do whatever I wanted without relying on my parents who were equally struggling to make ends meet. I later became a clerk dealing with customers and sponsors affairs. During the beginning of the year, we had to make sure all the accounting statements for the customers were true and fair. That meant we needed to work overtime especially when computers would be so slow. Some of my colleagues did not like that as they considered it to be too much work with just "a few coins to earn". Consequently some resigned. I knew at the bottom of my heart that this is the place God wanted me to serve Him. I knew how difficult it was to stay in the house with no job or any college to attend. So I treasured my job however tedious it was. Little did I know that just like any other place of work, there were office politics! Thank God for my naiveté.

After two years of service I thought I would get a permanent contract and that would imply a higher or better terms at work. The most painful bit is that with time, new employees would be employed without taking cognizant that I was there, serving diligently and all that. I purposed to be even more faithful to God. Hence, I served all the customers diligently and had a very good rapport with them. It was so amazing for me. For example, if a customer's statement had an error on the charges I would give them a definite date when they would come back to check and see if it had been corrected. As they queued I would call a customer by name and they would wonder how I knew them all by name. So they nicknamed me *"Doro"* and wanted to be served at my counter. That gave me fulfillment and a desire to continue serving them even better. With time, I noticed some customers had family problems that made them pay their bills late or some even required to be given some extension period to complete paying their bills. If it was a special case, I would carry all the proof to the Finance Manager to try and negotiate for a customer or a corporate customer so that they can be allowed to continue using the organization's services as they await funds. By the way these were customers who I had been serving before and so, I knew their financial status all through. God would cause me to be restless concerning their special cases. The cases were sometimes so difficult and would have to be forwarded to the Deputy Finance Director. Hence, some cases would be accepted while others would be rejected but I knew I had done my best after all. Somehow, I knew that policies were there to guide but not to break. Through this, as I kept taking needy cases to him, the Finance Manager recommended to the Finance Committee that customers and especially corporate customers be given an opportunity for paying their bills in installments. The Finance Committee obliged graciously.

One day, I went home to my mum and asked her "Mum I have worked for so long in the Finance Department but somehow when there is an opportunity for employment, others are employed and I don't even get an opportunity for an interview. How come no one ever thinks of recommending me for any post?" My mum would always rebuke me that I was not doing my best and that I had to wait for God to complete His good work through me. She taught me the story of Daniel that he was well favored, skilful in wisdom, had knowledge and ability to stand before the king's palace. Therefore, according to mum it meant I had to be excellent at work and pray that God gives me favor before the eyes of my bosses. According to Peterson (1997),

> "Having a good job does not mean that we will do it well. Having right roles does not guarantee righteousness. But having good work to do does not mean well to do good work. But no job is perfectly suited for carrying God's purposes. The key to living vocationally is being God called-spirit anointed. Saul failed but David succeeded yet both were kings of Israel" p.33.

After years of working as a casual, a new Finance Manager was employed. The first thing was to query why the Finance Office would have casual employees. I sensed that God had put a burden on this Finance Manager on our behalf. I was shortlisted, interviewed and got fulltime employment. Later on, I wrote a research paper on that organization that brought about changes that, the systems were reformed and everything was circulated to every employee to be aware of. During that time, it was so difficult but as I look at it now . . . perfection grows from one degree to another. Deuteronomy28 talks about the blessings that God gives to them that obey him. The Lord says He shall command a blessing in all that we do and we set our hands to do. He says he will bless **all** the work of our hands . . . That shows us that as children of God who believe that God has a good plan for us, He will surely bless all that we purpose to do with our hands. I have seen it come to pass. The same God of yesterday is the same God of today and will be the same in the future! Therefore, for those who might be wondering what their career is or even what God wants them to do with their lives, I would tell you to trust God that whatever you shall decide to do . . . God will bless it definitely. Do not fear . . . do not worry . . . just believe every word of God and claim it over your life, the fulfillment shall come to pass.

After some long period of working, a Senior Accountant whom we had worked together and was pleased with my work came to my office and told me, "Dorothy, you are so good with your work but if you do not go back to school, you shall remain in this same level doing the same thing over and over again. You have a lot of potential that you are not exploiting. Challenge yourself to go higher" That is what later I called bitter truth. It was difficult to accept it on that day but the same message kept ringing in my mind. She had set a spark in my life. Now what I needed was to fuel the spark! I started enquiring the possibility of doing a degree program although I had grown a little older! I started talking to friends and enquiring wherever and even checking different universities's websites for opportunities. I got to know of this university that has evening programme for mature students. The challenge was now back in my office, how I would convince the Finance Manager to give me a recommendation to get an employee development allowance that the organization had for its employees who personally developed themselves. There were so many of us who wanted to further their studies both professionally and academically. The benefit was dependent on the number of years each employee had worked. The more the number of years, the lesser the one had to bear the cost. I also think, if the boss was pleased with your work performance and they could see a future in you to the organization, the better your chance was. That was a good idea to try. My journey had begun . . .

Lessons learned:

❖ Be faithful and learn the job well as it will lead you to greater opportunities. Put your best foot forward. Do your very best; God sees and will reward your diligence. Isaiah48:17 says *"Thus says the Lord thy Redeemer, the Holy One of Israel; I am the Lord thy God which teacheth thee to profit which leadeth thee by the way that thou shouldest go (KJV).*

❖ Ask yourself whether what you are doing is God's calling for your life. One of the Joseph Prince Ministries 2013 Daily subscriptions': "Beloved, you must realize that very often, the battle is not without (in your external circumstances); it is within. The battle is in your mind and the battlefield, your beliefs and thoughts". *So just trust God like David in Psalms143:8 "Cause me to hear thy loving kindness in the morning; for in thee do I trust: cause me to know the way wherein I should walk; for I lift up my soul unto thee"* (KJV).

❖ There is something called "Divine Connection" that Solomon said in *Ecclesiastes 9:11 "I returned, and saw under the sun, that the race is not to the swift, nor the battle to the strong, neither yet bread to the wise, nor yet riches to men of understanding, nor yet favor to men of skill; **but time***

---

*__and chance happeneth to them all__" (*KJV*).* That shows everybody has an opportunity in life but when God leads your life then people call it a "coincidence" but to God there are no coincidences because He orders your steps. You are in the right place at the right time.

❖ It is not you . . . but God. Let go and let God work in you.

CHAPTER 3

Desire for Books

Definiteness of purpose is the starting point of all achievement.

W. Clement Stone

T he year I got my full time employment is the same year God blessed me with a sweet lovely husband. Am telling you when God says in Isaiah 61: 7 *"For your shame ye shall have double; and for confusion they shall rejoice in their portion: therefore in their land they shall possess the double: everlasting joy shall be unto them"* (KJV). My status had changed:

from a casual to a full time job, from being a single lady to being a married lady! My financial struggles at that time had come to an end. Another journey now began. God is and will always be faithful.

I shared with my husband my desire for going back to school. He was not only excited but very encouraging. In fact, he asked me: "What have you been doing working all these years without ever thinking of improving your credentials?" He is a graduate already from one of the top public university. Therefore, he suggested to me that it would be a good idea and the same time he would also consider doing a Master's degree. I applied and was privileged to be admitted and to study a Bachelor's Degree in Commerce through Continuing Education Program. The perk came with a condition of maintaining a GPA of 2.50 out the possible 4.00. Now, let's talk. I had been out of formal schooling for ten years. Wasn't this a very high calling? How would I do it? I had to multitask: work, study and family. That meant I had to work between 8:00 am to 5.00 pm then make sure I am in class by 5.30 pm to 8:30 pm, then find my way home. This wasn't easy. No pain no gain they aptly say. It was so tiring but I had to do it. Attendance was top priority as it was part of the grading system. After my first Continuous Assessment Test (CAT 1) when majority of the students got 30 marks out of 30; I got 6 marks out of 30. That I have never forgotten because I cried all the way home. I was so sad and wondered what was the reason of studying. Shouldn't I just give up? That particular evening when I met with my husband so that we go home together, he noticed I was quite sad. He asked me what the problem was. I told him; "I have failed my first CAT and I do not think I will be able to maintain the GPA of 2.50." When we arrived home and had had dinner we sat down together to strategize the way forward. My husband told me: "It seems after work you have no time to do your homework or revise what you have learned in the previous day. From today, we shall be leaving the house by 6.00 am and before you open your office to serve at 9.00 am ensure you have enough time to revise and catch up with what you studied earlier and it's going to be okay". We also agreed to be studying together at night and he promised to assist me with some theoretical concepts. I adhered to what we had agreed with my husband.

Later, God gave me some three treasured friends that I owe my achievement and love. We agreed that before we started our day at work we needed to pray. That truly worked miracles because by the end of that semester my GPA was not just 2.50/4.00 but 3.63/4.00. God is faithful, as you commit your life to seek Him, He will grant you what you ask of Him. He says in Matthew 6:33 *"But seek ye first the kingdom of God, and his righteousness; and all these things shall be added unto you."* Imagine God exactly means it. However, I made sure I attended all my classes; always did my assignments on time; and then asked God to grant me wisdom and knowledge to do my best. I had to record all these! I started noting in my diary what God was doing in my life. By the way, I still do keep a diary as evidence of what God does to me.

With all my studies, family and my work demands, I really needed God because I would not have made it without Him. After one year of my studies, the organization started facing financial challenges. Salaries were being delayed as well as creditors not being paid for their services. The Organization decided to downsize or to retrench the employees. It was a really difficult time among all employees. Losing a job is never easy. The gloomy mood was evident in the Organization as all asked quietly: "What will happen after I am laid off?" I was not an exemption, I got stressed. I knew without my job, my studies would come to an abrupt end. We couldn't have managed to raise my tuition fees notwithstanding the fact that my husband had also enrolled in a Post-Graduate program at another university. However, I knew one thing: God never aborts his plans concerning our lives especially if He was the one who had started it. I kept claiming and decreeing that God would not put me to shame. I reminded God how I never promised a student anything I could not deliver. I kept deadlines as well as kept promises in following up pending issues. I told Him to remember me like Hezekiah in the Bible that even when I was a casual, I remained faithful at my work. The retrenchment axe fell on many of my colleagues and because of my prayer and love from God, I was among the few that were retained. You know, that does not mean that God never loved the others but the way each of us viewed God depends. For example, Jesus had the multitude of disciples that followed Him, He also had the twelve disciples and an inner circle that sometimes accompanied Him like when He was being transfigured. But among all of them, even Simon Peter did not view God the way John did. John says he is the disciple whom Jesus loved. Okay! For me it was a confirmation that God has a good plan for my life.

Lesson the Heavenly Father taught me:

❖ The key to success is just to believe God! It is just as simple as it sounds. In the New Testament, the Bible shows how people were asking Jesus; what they must do to work the works of God? Jesus replied to them, that they believe on him whom he has sent. We only need to put our faith in Jesus Christ (John 6:28-29)

> ➢ Are you doing what God has called you to do or otherwise? The difference is that when doing what God has called you; even in the most difficult circumstances, somehow deep down your heart; you know God is with you and will not forsake you. There is a passion that keeps you going despite it all.

> ➢ If you wake up every morning complaining of the job that you are doing, seek God again concerning that job because GOD HATES MURMURING. Philippians 2:14 *"Do all things without murmuring and disputing. That ye may be blameless and harmless, the sons of God, without rebuke, in the midst of crooked and perverse nation, among whom ye shine as lights in the world"* (KJV)

➢ When success comes and you are celebrating God, the devil will always strike to see if you will curse God and forget His blessings upon you. However, Pastor Lee says "God tests our love for Him as he tested the children of Israelites. God proves himself and His blessing follow as He wants to show his power, sustenance and might to us. The story of the children of Israelites in Exodus 15: 21-27 elaborates this point *"And Miriam answered them, sing ye to the Lord, for he hath triumphed gloriously; the horse and his rider hath he thrown to the sea. So Moses brought Israel from the Red sea, and they went out into the wilderness of Shur; and they went three days in the wilderness, and found no water. And when they came to Marah, they could not drink of the waters of Marah, for they were bitter: therefore the name of it was called Marah. And the people murmured against Moses, saying what shall we drink? And he cried unto the Lord; and the Lord showed him a tree, which when he cast into the waters, the waters were made sweet: there he made for them an ordinance, and there he proved them. And said, if thou wilt diligently hearken to the voice of the Lord thy God, and wilt do that which is right in his sight, and wilt give ear to his commandments, and keep all his statutes, I will put none of these diseases upon thee, which I have brought upon Egyptians: for I am the Lord that healeth thee. And they came to Elim, where were twelve wells of water, and three score and ten palm trees: and they encamped there by the waters* (KJV).

➢ God's blessings are everlasting. They do not change. They are like a land mark in your life so that whenever doubt comes, the blessings will remind you of God's love. When those trying times come your way, always remember what God has already done for you and know He will still do it again. He is the same God, the creator who causes dawn to arise after a night has passed by. Night never remains forever, morning always must come by. Remember, even the darkest night has a dawn.

CHAPTER 4

Work Experience

I attribute my success to this: I never gave or took any excuse

Florence Nightingale

In Finance Office

After working for four years as a casual and four further years as a full time employee I had my hands-on on the job. I knew what to do and when to do it, and most important, what not to do. I am told that smooth seas do not produce tough sailors. This particular year of my job was quite an uphill task. One day, my direct supervisor and I were accused of swindling money from the Finance Office. This particular morning after Easter holiday, we arrived in the office and found our office was locked with a different key lock so that we would not get access. That morning, we got suspension letters with immediate notice that we go for compulsory leave as investigations start. This letter was sadly delivered to us by the security guard. Later, I was exempted from the compulsory leave but I was transferred to another branch as I was working in the Headquarters' office pending investigation. You can imagine, innocent as we were, this was it! We had been accused! By that time, we had really streamlined the customers and suppliers revenue and payment systems and policies. Ironically, we were so committed to our work that we sacrificed our sleep so that the system would be more efficient. Anyway we had to comply. My direct supervisor went home as I waited for the next bus to board and report to my new work place.

Just before that sad event, the company had just employed a new Chief Executive Officer who believed in encouraging and recognizing the best overall employees who were students and were attaining a GPA of 3.60 and above. To say the least, I was among those students. We had been taken for a luncheon in a five star hotel paid by the company as a way of motivating the top students. In his speech, the Chief Executive Officer had said that we needed to exemplify the same standards in our working areas.

Therefore, when I reported to my new work station, I was made the main cashier. One of the major job descriptions of that particular position is that I was the one to take the cheques for signing and approval to the Chief Executive Officer and the Deputy Finance Director. Later, I would take them to the bank, cash them then return back to the office and pay the concerned people. I wondered "I have been accused of swindling money via business transactions, how then can I be entrusted to handle real cash" For me that was a paradox. So, during lunch times or while I boarded the bus to go home, I would almost imagine people looking at me suspiciously in a manner likely to confirm . . . oh! That's the lady who stole money . . . that's the lady who was given a suspension letter . . . what is she still doing here? Apparently during this period, no one faced me directly to ask me what had happened. I went through a terrible time but this verse kept me sane. Psalms 109:1-4: *"Hold not thy peace o God of my praise; for the mouth of the wicked and the mouth of the deceitful are opened against me: they have spoken against me with a lying tongue. They compassed me about also with words of hatred; and fought against me without a cause. For my love they are my adversaries: but I give myself unto prayer."* My supervisor and I would call each other and we would say: "May God vindicate us" for I was sure something fishy was going on especially after I had voiced my concern.

One day I took the cheques to be signed by the Chief Executive Officer (CEO). The CEO saw my name on the cheque and asked the secretary to call me in. We had never met personally. When he saw me, he bluntly asked, "Young girl are you the one who is causing problems in Finance Office?" Immediately, God gave me courage to answer and I told him:" Sir, I have been working in the Finance Office for four years as a casual and now for the last four years I have been a full time employee, is this the time I should steal or then? I also attended the students' luncheon of the overall best students that was held last month and I heard you say that there is no way our job and grades can be different from the person. So I do not know what is happening to me now." I think the CEO was not expecting me to answer at all. He just looked at me in shock and did not ask me any other question. All I know is that investigations were completed and we were exonerated from the accusations. I went back to my former station while my supervisor was reinstated back to her office. Thank God for the leadership of the then CEO and Deputy Finance Director for seeking God in that matter. I know many other people were praying for the same. Praise the Lord! There is a comment that most people use: the greater the challenge the greater the blessing. The same year 2005, I graduated as the best overall academic student of the year. Can you imagine, the same person who was wondering whether she would achieve the minimum GPA of 2.5, now graduating as the best student with the highest GPA? Isn't God faithful?

Once again . . . the same year, I was blessed with a beautiful baby girl. (Didn't I share with you about God's grace? His blessings come in doubles!!!). Just to mention here, since we had gotten married, it had taken four years into our marriage without a baby. For those who know the African culture, children are so important and are a great blessing to a family. Some people also think that children are a source of wealth for the family. We had been visiting various doctors to get opinions of why we could not have children. The final doctor who is the best in that area told me that my fallopian tubes had been blocked and I could not be able to conceive. We used to pray every day beseeching God to bless us with a baby. Life was so devastating that I hated anyone whether at work or at home asking me, "What are you waiting for?" To me, I was like, *"Am I the one who creates children . . . you remember the story of Jacob and Rachel. Rachel told Jacob in Genesis 30 to give her children or else she dies. Jacob's anger increased and answered her "Am I in God's stead, who hath withheld from thee the fruit of your womb?"* (Verse 2, KJV). So why is everyone asking me all these questions . . . we were trying to have children but the children were not coming . . ." Later, I took time to go and seek God over my life . . . While I was praying, God told me that He would bless me with a baby girl and I would call her blessing. So, the same year I was facing all these problems at my work place, I had just conceived and was four months into pregnancy. I was praising God and thanking Him for remembering me yet again. The devil is a liar since he was trying my faith desperately at my work area.

Travelling by the company's bus was no mean feat. It took over one hour to get to work. Some sections of the road were rough, bumpy, and dusty and with a few diversions, the journey was not very interesting for a pregnant lady. I told myself, nothing by passes God or gets God by surprise. He works with a master plan. If He had allowed me to go through what I was going through, He would enable me to be a victor. I kept talking and validating myself. "I can do it! I can do it!" Many times I cried to God . . . I knew the devil was mad that I had conceived . . . I knew he wanted to do anything to cause me to be angry and curse God. But I remained silent. I knew after a victorious situation in my life, the devil always passes behind my back. I told myself . . . God is faithful. My baby shall grow well. At eight months, I got gestational diabetes and the baby threatened to come out prematurely. I was hospitalized for a week. That time, my mum fasted and prayed for me as I got encouragement from friends and family. My husband walked with me through it all. Hence, all these time bad things were happening to me, I knew God would take me to sustenance soon. The story of the children of Israelites about God providing in the middle of trouble (wilderness), I knew He would do it to me too. I mean the essence of why we read the word of God every day is for us to use it to claim God's promises. They are precious and exceedingly great so that we may be able to escape corruption that is in the world through lust (1st Peter1:4). I remembered my dad's favorite verse in Psalms 34:6 *"This poor man cried and the Lord heard him, and saved him out of all his troubles"* (KJV). In God's time, my daughter was born. My husband never left my side no matter what. The baby was born in his presence. The first person I wanted to talk to was my mum. I called her and asked her, "Mum! Did you have to go through what I have just undergone for the five of us?" She only laughed. Again I asked her, "Mum! Did I used to answer you when you called my name or did I used to do whatever you asked me to do?" Again, she only laughed. Then I knew the verse that talks about children honoring parents and parents not provoking their children to anger . . . Wow! Amazing! Bishop T.D. Jakes says "There are some things only age can teach you"

One year later, as a way of God wiping my tears He gave me favor by granting me a promotion in the office. In addition, I applied the same university for a Master's Programme. I also got to know from the university that there were scholarship being granted to the overall best student. I applied and by God's grace I received His favor and I was granted a Vice Chancellor Scholarship to pursue my post graduate studies. This is what God can do to them that trust Him. He is faithful. As I said earlier, I have a sweet, supporting husband. Sometimes over the weekend I would need to go for discussion group with my fellow classmates. My husband's car boot was a baby's moving house. He carried diapers, baby's food and toys. He was and has been such a supporting husband. I would never have done this without his help. Sometimes, he would have to go to the library to pick and drop books for me; he would wait for me in the evening to pick me after class; he would sit at night waiting for me to finish my assignments and proof read them. When I was writing my thesis paper, he helped me in editing, printing, and sometimes picking it from my supervisor. In two years I was able to finish my postgraduate degree. Thanks to my husband and it was an honor to graduate with a cumulative high GPA of 3.79/4.00.

That year, as I was graduating, sadly our country was going through a terrible time with tribal and ethnic clashes precipitated by elections that were allegedly rigged. Neighbors who had earlier lived as friends were raising pangas (machetes) on each other. The consequences of that was death, displacement of people, and much more high inflation and a drop to our economic growth. This meant that institutions and organization were trying to cut down on their expenses and running costs. In the midst of all these, again I found favor with God. I got a new job in the midst of all these and appointed in one of the best private universities as a Graduate Assistant in the Department of Commerce. At the same time, we were blessed with a baby boy.

I remember when I was six months pregnant, my Head of Department together with me, had organized for an International field trip to Egypt, Jordan and Dubai. I had to accompany the students. I remember so well going up to Mount Sinai. For those who have gone to this mountain, you know they are very steep all the way to the peak. Once you are at the top, there is a beautiful sunset and I wanted to see it before dawn. I am telling you, up to today; I do not know how I managed to climb that mountain and go to the top. I can only say God is an awesome God. To make things even better, I also went for the Dubai sand dunes drives in the desert that is usually done using land cruisers vehicles. Talk of the goodness of the Lord. No harm came to me, I did not even vomit as the students did yet I was pregnant!

When the time of life came for the baby to be born it was a miracle baby. This is because I was expecting for the water to break like it had happened to my daughter. Instead of the water breaking I felt a bit of discomfort then, I called a friend of mine who was a nurse and told me to go to the hospital urgently. After a few hours she called me back and asked how I was doing. The moment I mentioned to her that I had not yet gone to the hospital, she became so furious with me and asked me why I was behaving so ignorantly despite the command to go to the hospital. Since I had visited my best couple's house I requested her to immediately drop me to the hospital. As soon as we arrived in the hospital the doctor looked at me and said "you are in labour" How did he know . . . I was not in pain but I called my husband to tell him I was in the hospital not sure what was happening to me. The doctor broke the water and exactly after 35minutes a baby boy was born. From when my son was young, he loves riding the roller coasters, jumping from such high tops and is an excited boy. I agree with pediatricians who encourage mothers or fathers to talk to the baby while still in the womb, they will recognize your voice once the baby is born. Also, it is good to know what we do when pregnant; it has a direct effect on the baby. Wow!

Lessons Learned:

❖ If you hear your friend or neighbor or colleague has been involved in a particular scandal and you have not talked to that person to confirm the facts or you do not have the facts, just keep quiet. Learn to bridle your tongue. God hates a double minded person. Psalms12: 2-3 *"They speak vanity everyone with his neighbor: with flattering lips and with a double heart do they speak. The Lord shall cut off all flattering lips, and the tongue that speaketh proud things."* Romans 13:8 *"Owe no man anything, but to love one another: for he that loveth another has fulfilled the law"* (KJV).

❖ Sometime when there are couples around you who have been married for a couple of years and have no children, the best gift you can give them is prayers. Do not pester them with questions about why they are not having children. If it is not out of choice, it only hurts them more; it is like adding salt to an injury.

❖ Dignity is inherent at work. Be faithful even in the little matters. This is what integrity really is. As a rule, train yourself that wherever you go, leave it better than you found it. This calls for self-discipline. Even when you think your boss should have recognized you for your effort but doesn't, God does. His payment plan is better than your boss's. Philippians 3:19-21 *"And to know the love of Christ, which passeth knowledge, that ye might be filled with all the fullness of God. Now unto him that is able to do exceeding abundantly above all that we ask or think, according to the power that worketh in us, unto him be glory in the church by Christ Jesus throughout all ages, world without end Amen"* (KJV)

❖ Even when it is your right to get something, do not complain or grumble. You need to talk about it. There is a difference between talking and complaining. The children of Israel when in the wilderness they grumbled to Moses about lack of water and food. God sent fiery snakes that bit the people and many of them died (Numbers21:5)

In Lecturer Room

Even if, I had worked in a Finance Office for 10 years, I had the experience, the grades and what it takes to be a lecturer but I did not know how to stand in front of my students and teach. I remember my first day in class, after I introduced myself and got to know the students names, I got so nervous, sweaty and confused. I couldn't go on. I was so ashamed and discouraged that I felt that I needed to go back to the Head of Department and tell him that I cannot do this. Being a lecturer seemed so difficult compared to working in the office despite the late nights. However, I thank God that he was out of the country on a business trip. If you remember, I had mentioned earlier in the first chapter that I swore never to be a teacher because everybody in my family was a teacher! It took God to minister to me through a Pastor friend of mine . . . . who reminded me the story of Gideon. When God came to Gideon in Judges 6:14-16 *"And the Lord looked upon him and said, Go in this thy might, and thou shalt save Israel from the hand of the Midianites; have I not sent thee? And he said unto him, Oh my Lord, wherewith shall I save Israel? Behold my family is poor in Manasseh, and I am the least in my father's house. And the Lord said unto him, Surely I will be with thee, and thou shalt smite the Midianites as one man"*(KJV).

I got encouraged and asked God to really help me. I kept whispering to myself that I can do it. Whatever the Management Board saw in me, Lord, let me also be hopeful that it shall come to pass. Confidence belongs to God and God will not put me to shame." I had memorized a short verse in Psalms 34:9 *O fear the Lord, ye his saints: for there is no want to them that fear him."* I went to share with my mentor about all these challenges I was facing. By the way, "the higher you go the cooler it becomes." I got to know that phrase better." When I told her what happened in class, she laughed to tears. She later explained to me that she had had a similar experience when she started teaching. She told me not to worry, it was just a matter of time. She literally taught me how to stand in front of the students, how to use the white board and generally how to teach. It is so hard when you know what to say but somehow the words cannot come out of your mouth. She was such a blessing to me both at school and at my personal life. I am also grateful to another lecturer who was so good in teaching English language in the university. She taught me how to prepare lessons plans. It was so hard at that time but I promised myself I must do it. A few months later, I started enjoying teaching especially after seeing the enthusiasm of my students. I got a new perspective of my life. I also started attending seminars on teaching and how to relate better with my students in the Collaboration for Excellence in Teaching and Learning (CETL). The seminars were so effective and refreshing.

After two years I was appraised in my work and confirmed as an Assistant Lecturer. That year, I organized an International field trip to the USA for two weeks with the collaboration of a Private University in the US. It was such a blessed trip as the business students had an experience of visiting some of the best 500 famous companies awarded in the Fortune Magazine. In these companies they could relate theory and practicability. It was a wonderful time as we heard many CEOs talk to our students and challenge them of their thinking in a global working environment. Not just to focus in one area as with many countries have reduced trading barriers that used to be there. Other CEOs shared their lives as a testimony to show the students that there is nothing impossible if you have faith. For me, that CEO was my hero as I could identify with her.

Nonetheless, when I was attending a seminar at CETL I saw an announcement of an upcoming Conference on Council of Christian Colleges and Universities asking for anyone interested to write a research on gender and work. I thought that was an interesting topic to research on especially in my life. I had just met a super woman who was doing what other people thought she could not do. I also wanted to know how the results would be from my University that represents majority from the world and from Africa. Therefore, I wrote and sent an abstract which they accepted. It was so interesting to do a research out of my own interest. I appreciated the pressure I got when I was doing my Master's research paper. Anyway, God was so gracious that I got a sponsorship out of the University's budget and went to present my paper in Abilene, USA in an International Conference.

It was my first conference in my life as I had an honor to meet with recognized professors, academicians of note, field practitioners and students in the US. Most of the attendees were from the US and only two of us were from Africa. I listened to the issues that were presented from the various Universities. I could not keep quiet. I challenged them that they needed to appreciate their Universities as African universities were much more less than what they had received. The key speaker challenged us as academicians that if we do not do research we shall become irrelevant in our profession. Furthermore, pursuing a PhD is just a basic tool that each facilitator requires. I decided that I needed to be the best faculty in the area of my study by striving to pursue a PhD. In addition, the following month a survey conducted by Commission of Higher Education (CHE) in Kenya showed 'there is an acute shortage of professors at a time when higher education sub sector is experiencing exponential growth.'(Daily Nation, November 6th 2010). Therefore, my pursuit of a Ph.D would go a long way in meeting that challenge and be counted as a solution to enhance the set goals by CHE.

Lesson learned:

❖ When you are weak spiritually, that is when you are strong. God uses you when you least expect so that all the glory will belong to Him.

❖ Currently, information is power. Whenever possible make sure you are in touch with your company or organization's endeavors. Many times employees miss out on an opportunity because they even did not know what is happening. Some opportunities come about when you are willing to go an extra mile. Just try that!

❖ Oh! I thank God for my University that has been a blessing to me. If I would be asked yet again if I would like to serve and work there, I would still say "Yes"! Luke16:12 argue us *"And if ye have not been faithful in that which is another man's who shall give you that which is your own? No servant can serve two masters: for either he will hate the one, and love the other; or else he will hold to the one, and despise the other. Ye cannot serve God and mammon."* KJV

❖ When you desire anything from God, believe and then start preparing yourself to receive it by faith. The faster you see it coming to pass the faster what you were hoping for becomes a reality. For faith is an evidence of things hoped for. When you have a conviction in your heart concerning doing something, just go for it. Taking students to the USA was something that was beyond my wildest dreams. To my students, it was like the biggest dream come true. Isaiah43:19 says, *"Behold, I will do a new thing; now it shall spring forth; shall ye know it? I will even make a way in the wilderness, and rivers in the desert."* (KJV)

CHAPTER 5

Dream Come True: In Pursuant of a PhD

Twenty years from now you will be more disappointed by the things that you

didn't do than by the ones you did do, so throw off the bowlines, sail away from

safe harbor, catch the trade winds in your sails. Explore, Dream, Discover.

Mark Twain

B eyond any reasonable doubt, I wanted to do my PhD abroad to experience a different exposure finances notwithstanding. God had already taken me far enough for me to trust in Him. I started thinking about a research topic that I would be interested in writing. With the help of my colleagues, I was able to draft a proposal.

At the same time, a good friend of mine (Dot) passed on and left behind two children. Her demise was extremely devastating to me. Life took a different turn. So many friends and relatives have passed on before but for one reason or another, this was a blow to me; it affected me a great deal. I think God was sending a message for me. This is because nothing was making sense to me at that time . . . How can my friend just leave us so soon. I started contemplating resigning from work to take care of my children. Apparently, in our places of work, we only mourn with the departed for just but a moment and life has to go on. But it is never the same for the deceased family. So I thought the best thing I would do was for me to resign from work and go home to take care of my children so that they would appreciate the time we spend together. That is the greatest job that God has given to us as mothers. I called my elder sister to tell her of my upcoming plans. The words she told me keep ringing in my mind. Ephesians 1:17 *"That the God of our Lord Jesus Christ, the Father of glory, may give unto you the spirit of wisdom and revelation in the knowledge of him"* (KVJ)

That following week just before the burial, God started teaching me about resurrection and why the Gospel is so powerful. One day as I was teaching I did not have the strength to continue, I gave my students some 30 minutes of assignments as I went to the lounge to relax since I was so restless. I told God, "You must reveal to me the purpose of my life. I need to know so that I can serve you better." The Lord's faithfulness is real. He reminded me of my life since high school, how He has been providing for me in difficult situations, what He has been doing through me in my work place, in my marriage and He is not yet finished with me. I immediately felt that I needed to read God's word in 1st Corinthians 15. The whole chapter deals with the resurrection. It shows the reason why Christ came on earth to die for us and save us from our sins. In addition, the words are encouraging to the Christians on the purpose of resurrection. Now what struck me most was the last verse of the chapter *"Therefore, my beloved brethren, be ye steadfast, unmoveable, always abounding in the work of the Lord, for as much as ye know that your labour is not in vain in the Lord"* (Vs. 58 KVJ). Many difficult situations will come our way but Jesus urges us to stand still. We should not allow the circumstances or happenings to move us around since life is not stable. But in all these happenings remain still in the Lord and let him direct our ways.

There and then, I knew God was calling me to serve in my university and to be a blessing to my students. There is no greater thing in my life like when I see the satisfaction of my students. It brings the greatest joy for me to be there for them. Immediately the Lord gave me a word also in Hebrews 8:11-12 *"For this is the covenant that I will make with the house of Israel after those days, saith the Lord; I will put my laws into their mind, and write them in their hearts: and I will be to them a God, and they shall be to me a people: And they shall not teach every man his neighbor, and every man his brother, saying know the Lord: for all shall know me, from the least to the greatest. For I will be merciful to their unrighteousness, and their sins and their iniquities will I remember no more"* (KJV).

For sure, I knew God is going to be the best steward of my children no matter what. There is nothing I can do without His help . . . I needed not resign. The students are my new assignment and I need to mentor them better than I have been doing. Being concerned about my own children is just but a small thing. He who sacrifices all (money, children, parents, wealth, power, family) for the sake of Jesus Christ he/she shall find them.

God has been watching over me and my children all this time as I have travelled to more than ten countries leaving them very young under God's care. What is it that He cannot do? His words affirm that he/she who casts his/her bread upon many waters shall find it after many days (Ecclesiastes 11:1). I knew what God has spoken He would do it for me . . . He reminded how He watched over me while climbing Mt. Sinai with a six month pregnancy . . . This God is able . . . so I was not scared at all.

God will teach my children to say no to sin and how to love God as He had given me a word already. He would be merciful and forgive their sins. In Job 1:4-5 *"And his sons went and feasted in their houses, everyone his day; and sent and called for their three sisters to eat and to drink with them. And it was so, when the days of their feasting were gone about, that job sent and sanctified them, and offered burnt offering according to the number of them all: for job said, it may be that my sons have sinned, and cursed God in their hearts. Thus did job continually"*. Therefore if the law having a shadow of good things allowed the priests to stand for man in the presence of God in the sanctuary and could never go to the Holies of Holies without blood . . . how much more shall the blood of Christ purge our conscience from dead works to serve the living God? (Hebrews 9 and 10).Therefore nothing can separate us (the children of God) from the love of God. He further confirmed it again in Hebrews10:16-17 *"This is the covenant that I will make with them after those days, saith the Lord, I will put my laws into their hearts, and in their minds will I write them; And their sins and iniquities will I remember no more"* (KJV). After that, I went immediately to class and taught so enthusiastically and I knew God was in control. Later, when I was in the bus travelling home after work I meditated on that word and knew God has a good plan for my life. I knew why God in the first place ever created me.

Sometime later, the department of Quality Assurance circulated an email of an organization that was looking for young academicians and scientists to sponsor. I knew this was the opportunity I had asked God for and it had come. I sent an abstract which was accepted for a day's training on how to write a good PhD proposal. The greatest challenge I had was to search for a professor who was willing to supervise my work. If I would get one, then he/she would commit in writing so that I could be admitted in that particular University he/she was attached to. I got one professor, but he later turned me down because he was doing the same kind of research with another student. He told me it would be a conflict of interest. However, I had attended an interview for the scholarship. By the end of the year, I got a call from the Chairman that I did not succeed. That was really heart breaking! I cried to God with such a heavy heart and felt like I had been forsaken. God, for one year I was pursuing this and I knew it would be successful, why now? Anyway, I was like if I would have gotten the scholarship I would have been so thankful, so I said to myself that I need to be thankful to God despite. I lifted my hands while in my living room and thanked God for the opportunity I had gotten despite being turned down. I told God "I choose to trust you even when it does not make sense". I asked Him to show me what to do next. For sure once again God's faithfulness is eternal.

An idea came to my mind on some call for papers that had been circulated from various parts of the world. I thought that was something I would pursue since there was nothing to lose. All I was claiming in my heart was that the following year, by September I needed to be in class doing my PhD. I wrote the two abstracts and sent them to the various places. January the following year, I got news that both the abstracts had been accepted and I needed to finish the full papers by March. With the help of my husband with proof reading and my younger sister and my Cousin who helped me collect data and key it into the computer, I was set to go. I was quite busy I did not know how time passed by. That time, since I had the experience of being an Accountant, I used to follow our School of Business and Economics budget. Information is power as I said . . . I got to know the year was coming to an end and all the funds allocated to various departments would be returned to the kitty and re-allocated to the needful departments. Therefore, I applied for funding from my department to present my paper out of the country. I got favor with the Vice Chancellor, the Deputy Vice Chancellor, the Dean and my Head of Department. I went to present my paper in International Business School's conference.

After returning, there was also another mail circulated about another scholarship. I told myself, I am not going to give up. I must try this as it looks like my prayers are going to be answered! It was such a short span of a weekend to complete the application and recommendation requirements and submit all the documents by Monday 8:00 am. I wondered if really this part of the world had such a scholarship. I had never heard or thought of it. There is a story in the Bible when Jesus was calling His disciples; one asked . . . what good can come out of Nazareth? Thank God I had all my documents on my desktop while I was applying the first scholarship that had not materialized. I filled all the application forms as required and got my recommendation letter and by Monday everything was ready. I went to present my second paper that my abstract had been accepted as I also waited for the results of the scholarship. This time, instead of going out the country, the conference location was changed to where I was. That was so amazing because this time I did not have funds to travel. I just had to organize the registration and bus travelling funds. I would then go home to sleep after the day's presentation. After three months. I received news that my name was among those who had received the scholarship to go and study.

This time my brother Peter Muthoka and I were studying the book of Ezra together. When this scholarship came, I was studying Ezra 7: 18-20 *"And whatsoever shall seem good to thee, and to thy brethren, to do with the rest of the silver and gold, that do after the will of your God. The vessels also that are given thee for the service of the house of thy God, those deliver thou before the God of Jerusalem. And whatsoever more shall be needful for the house of thy God, which thou shalt have occasioned to bestow, bestow it out of the king's treasure house."* Praise the Lord, the blessings of the Lord addeth no sorrow. In that year, September as I had claimed, I left for my studies and was in class doing my PhD program . . . Amen!!!

Lessons learned:

❖ Always confess positively what you want in your life and claim it no matter what. Bishop T. D. Jakes says "Anytime God promises you something, get ready for trouble. The enemy will always attempt to oppose the word of God spoken over your life".

❖ What you want in life, start preparing it by faith because God honors faith! I got to learn that in the book of John. Before Jesus went to the cross, He prayed for us many times that whatsoever we want to ask of the Father through Jesus's Name he would give it unto us . . . whatsoever means ANYTHING we need . . . and He shall do it. We just need to believe that He hears and knows all that we need at all times. No wonder the Lord's Prayer is all about asking . . . the right asking . . .

o John15:16 *"Ye have not chosen me, but I have chosen you, and ordained you, that ye should go and bring forth fruit, and that your fruit should remain: That whatsoever ye shall ask of the Father in my name, he may give it you"*(KJV)

o John16:23 *"And in that day ye shall ask me nothing. Verily, verily, I say unto you, whatsoever ye shall ask the Father in my name, he will give it you"*(KJV)

---

o John16:24 *"Hirtherto have ye asked nothing in my name: ask and ye shall receive that your joy may be full"* (KJV)

o John16:26 *"At that day ye shall ask in my name: and I say not unto you, that I will pray the Father for you:"*(KJV).

❖ Never give up even when the circumstances are showing impossibility. "Abraham, the Bible says, never staggered away from his promise despite the number of years and it came to pass . . . we also can do it . . . gonna believe. Job in the midst of what he was going through was confident that *"for I know that my redeemer liveth, and that he shall stand at the latter day upon the earth: And though after my skin worms destroy this body, yet in my flesh shall I see God"* Job19:25-26 (KJV).

❖ I bless the Lord for such organizations that have a burden to bless students who have the capabilities but have no funds. May God bless the leadership of these organizations that they may fulfill their vision by granting many more opportunities to various students in the world!

❖ 1 John 5:14-15: This is the confidence we have in approaching God, that if we ask anything according to His will, he hears us.

❖ Read the testimonies below as evidence of what God can do.

DETERMINED TO SUCCEED

by Wanjiru Mwangi

A staunch believer in taking every opportunity that comes her way, Dorothy Kagwaini chanced at the opportunity to represent Daystar University at the Council for Christian Colleges and Universities (CCCU) in Messiah College, USA.

While studying the book, *Creating Significant Learning Experiences: An Integrated Approach to Designing College Courses by L. Dee Fink* during Daystar faculty curriculum development study group and writers forum, Dorothy came across a call for presentations organized by CCCU. Going by the theme *Changing Faces: Changing Opportunities & Campus Climates for Women & Men*, the conference aimed at addressing gender issues for students, faculty, staff, and administrators.

Determined to be part of this conference, Dorothy sought advice from Prof. Faith Nguru, Dean School of Communication, Languages and Performing Arts on a viable topic write on, and settled for the work-family issues. To meet the deadline of April 19th 2010, Dorothy set off researching and interviewing staff and faculty of Daystar University, and finally submitted her proposal, *Work-Family Issues: A Case of Daystar University*. As a mother, wife and professional, Dorothy often wondered whether staff and faculty members were able to separate work and family issues, or if they overrode each other. *My presentation addressed the challenges of juggling marriage, family and singleness with roles in academia within the university*", said Dorothy. "*I wanted to understand whether it is easy to block one part of one's life and concentrate on another without getting destructed*".

Anyone who has spent time with Dorothy can agree with me that she is very passionate about what she does. Dorothy gave her all to ensure that her proposal was up to par. Her face lights up as she narrates the day she received the email, confirming that she had been selected to present her paper at the *Changing Faces* Conference. "*It was a privilege to attend the conference and as the only Kenyan, I was honoured to represent my country and Daystar University*," said Dorothy.

The conference which was held at Abilene Christian University (ACU), September 29-October brought together representative from ACU, Bethel University, Calvin College, Point Loma Nazarene University, and Trinity Western University. More than 100 female and male faculty and administrators from across the United States, Canada, and Kenya attended the conference. Only two of the presenters were from Africa, representing Kenya and Nigeria. Concerned about the low participation from African countries, Dorothy says, *"For a continent that is greatly affected by gender and family issues, I was surprised by the low participation of African institutions. I look forward to another opportunity and hope that my colleagues will join in representing Africa to the World".*

Dorothy's determination to succeed is unwavering. Having began as a casual at Daystar's Finance office, Dorothy was looked down upon because she was uneducated. She had the desire to pursue a degree, but lacked the financial support. She later received a scholarship and graduated as the best student of the year in a double major of Accounting and Business Administration. For an achiever, one degree was not enough and she later enrolled for her masters. Dorothy believes in always having a positive attitude, "To a valiant heart, nothing is impossible. Attitude has a lot to do with where one wants to be in life. It not only determines the future, but it also affects where we are today and the decisions we make," says Dorothy. After attending the CCCU's gender conference, I am not the same. I look forward to pursuing my Ph.D. so that I can have more impact on my students.

In her conclusion, Dorothy quotes from Marilyn Carlson Nelson's book, *How We Lead Matters: Reflection on a Life of Leadership*, where she says, *"If you look at each stage of your life as an opportunity to make a difference, your effectiveness will increase, your reputation will grow and extraordinary possibilities will present themselves. In the end, you weren't really dreaming about titles or position or even about being a wife/ mother. Rather you were dreaming about having the life that would complete you."* Today, she is a faculty member making an impact on her students as she encourages them that they can be whatever they want to be. However, this does not come on a silver platter. It takes commitment and discipline.

Dorothy Muthoka Kagwaini is a Lecturer in the School of Business and Economics.

Women in the Hall

By

Dorothy Muthoka

Currently, women have made strides in the field of leadership despite many difficulties in the stereotypical male-dominated world. It is always interesting to read and listen to life experiences of women who have made it in leadership against all odds. Pastor Cathy Kiuna in her book, *Woman Without Limit,* says with astounding finality that "a woman of character prefers to associate herself with people that will draw her closer to God." There are times when trouble comes and the only hope and answer is to trust the Most High God. God has and will always be the driving force behind many a woman's success. According to Psalm 91 (NIV), "He who dwells in the shelter of the Most High will rest in the shadow of the Almighty." That is where I chose to dwell as I briefly write how far the Lord has brought me.

There were times I was looked down on as uneducated because I lacked fees to go to college although I had passed my high school. The desire to continue with university education was there, but financial limitations had seemingly crippled that endeavor. While working at the revenue section of the finance department, my supervisor was sacked, and I was the only lady then in the section available to take up the position. However, I was turned down since I was unqualified for the job. I felt discouraged at that moment, but I took it up as a challenge to my career life. To a valiant heart, nothing is impossible. Attitude has a lot to do with where one wants to be in life. It not only determines the future, but it also affects where we are today and the decisions we make. That was the propelling force that made me enrol for a degree course, Bachelor of Commerce in Accounting and Business Administration, at Daystar University in order to pursue my dream career.

This decision, like many others, came with a myriad of challenges. It was very difficult having to sustain a busy daily schedule of an 8:00 a.m.-5:00 p.m. job then attending classes 5:30 p.m.-8:30 p.m. I am fortunate to have a supportive and understanding husband who not only motivated me to study but also helped in house chores. I always purposed never to go to class with unfinished assignments and to also always be the best at serving students during my office work. Talk of balance! After the long academic journey that almost scarred my social life, God rewarded my deeds by helping me graduate as the best student of the year, both in my school and among all the university's graduates. My dream changed and I wanted to be the best there can ever be at Daystar University.

Before my undergraduate studies, I never thought that I would even dream of studying beyond a first degree. Now I had another desire: to take a master's degree. I expanded my horizons. Immediately, I joined the Graduate School for my M.B.A. Again, the road wasn't easy with a young, tender family, a job and my studies. I remember one day holding my baby on one side as I did my take-home assignments. Again, I had to balance! This led to questions from my children: "Mum, do you sleep at school?" This, I guess, was due to the fact that I would get home late while the children were asleep and leave very early in the morning before they woke up. But God is and will always remain faithful. As hard as it seemed, I had to create time for them, especially on Sundays.

Marilyn Carlson Nelson in her book, *How We Lead Matters: Reflection on a Life of Leadership*, says, "If you look at each stage of your life as an opportunity to make a difference, your effectiveness will increase, your reputation will grow and extraordinary possibilities will present themselves. In the end, you weren't really dreaming about titles or position or even about being a wife/mother. Rather you were dreaming about having the life that would complete you." Today, I am a faculty member making an impact on my students as I encourage them that they can be whatever they want to be. However, this does not come on a silver platter. It takes commitment and discipline.

The best thing is when they ask me whether I started as low as a casual student in Daystar University. I always encourage and challenge them that they can make it and be what they desire to be especially before the challenges of being mum or wife knock on their lives. After attending the CCCU's recent gender conference at Abilene Christian University, I am not the same. I look forward to pursuing my Ph.D. so that I can have more impact on my students.

CHAPTER 6

Shocking News

The two most important days in your life are the day

you are born and the day you find out why

Mark Twain

S ometime in the course of the year, I felt that I had missed my youngest brother, who was working in a different city from where I was working. I had not seen him for almost a year. I asked my husband if I would go for five days to visit him as I was having a semester break for two weeks.

He obliged. I went and spent a wonderful time with my brother in May. He would come home from work and find I had already prepared dinner for him. Oh! It was such an amazing time. We agreed that in July he would pay us a visit especially due to the fact that our children were constantly asking me that they would want to see 'uncle Kyallo' as they fondly called him. After one week, my brother started complaining of sharp stomach pains. Being single, my mum went to stay with him (talk of the love of a mother). She took him to hospital and was given anti-malaria tablets (this is a very common disease in Africa). Within a few days my brother was unable to eat well and he was getting worse. He became so weak that my mum became so worried about his health. Later, mum was advised to take him to a specialist to diagnose what was happening to him. The doctor diagnosed that he was suffering from Pneumonia—a rare disease in that region of the country because it is always hot. He was scheduled for an immediate operation that went successfully. Later, my brother could not breathe well and on June 21st my brother passed on. This was a cold day for us as a family. Gone too soon we cried. It seems God loved him more than us!

The news was disclosed to me through a phone call on my way to work. That day I had two three hour classes. Surprisingly to all and sundry, I was very strong somehow. Everybody in my family and friends was telling me that I had not accepted what had happened. But little did they know that the previous year I had mourned so much for my friend Dot and that God had taught me about the resurrection and trusting in Him. 2 Corinthians 5:7-10 *"Therefore we are always confident, knowing that, whilst we are at home in the body, we are absent from the Lord: (For we walk by faith, not by sight ;) We are confident, I say, and willing rather to be absent from the body and to present or absent, we may be accepted of him. For we must all appear before the judgment seat of Christ; that everyone may receive the things done in his body, according to that he hath done, whether it be good or bad"* (KJV). It did not make sense to them but I knew what God had taught me and I needed to trust Him especially when it was most difficult or when it didn't seem to make sense. He for sure was and is always faithful . . . He held me through till after the burial and up to today. Thank God I had been able to spend time with my brother—had I not obeyed it would have been so devastating for me. I learned Ephesians 3: 19-20" *And to know the love of Christ, which passeth knowledge, that ye might be filled with all fullness of God. NOW to him that is able to do exceeding abundantly above all that we ask or think according to the power that worketh in us"* (KJV). Love is powerful; it forgives, it perseveres, it's humble, it does not boast, if I become filled with that fullness of God (love) whatever I think Jesus is able to do it. That was amazing to comprehend.

Sadly some of us get so busy with life issues that we don't hear God's calling about a loved one. It may be that call, visit, or a text that would make a difference. The greatest resource we have in our disposal is time . . . yet it is like gold. We run after so many things that sometimes are not a priority. God gave us life to enjoy it and know God's kingdom in heaven is the same on earth.

By and by I learned my lesson:

❖ To enjoy the time God gives you to be here on earth. Life is too short to harbor grudges. For Psalms 90: 9 says *"For all our days are passed away in thy wrath: we spend our years a tale that is told."* Instead we should number our years *and that knowing the time, that now it is high to awake from out of sleep: for now is our salvation nearer than when we believe. The night is far spent, the day is at hand: not in rioting and drunkenness, not in chambering and wantonness, not in strife and envying. But put ye on the Lord Jesus Christ* (Romans13:11-14) (KJV).

❖ Always keep promises and if you be not in a position to fulfill, please make sure you call and excuse yourself . . . especially in this age of digital communication! There is no excuse for not keeping your word. If not, then do not promise things that are beyond your reach. Jesus cautioned the New Testament believers that the least you do to these my brethren you do it unto me. God is a covenant keeping God and so because we are His children; we should also be covenant keeping children.

❖ Treasure each other. Know who you are. You do not have to prove who you are to people. When Jesus was taken

---

before Pilate and people mocked him, slapped him, beat him, and crucified him, He was silent all through. Many wanted Him to prove that He was Jesus the King. But that is why He defeated the devil. At the appointed time, the centurion confessed He was Christ. Then, if Jesus knew He was a Son of God, He did not have to prove himself; why do you try proving yourself unnecessarily? The people who prove themselves have a problem with their self-esteem and many times they manipulate others. Don't you know that God has made you kings and priests to reign on the earth? (Revelation 5:10) You are a child of God. You reign with Christ. You are a co-heir in the kingdom of God. Come out of your identity crisis. Your words are life. Speak carefully, however with confidence and power that is in you.

❖ When difficult times come your way and you are wondering why? Remember the sovereignty of God. Psalms 115: 1-2 tell us *"Not unto us, o Lord, not unto us, but unto thy name give glory, for thy mercy, and for thy truth's sake. Wherefore should the heathen say where their God is now?"*(KJV). Do not fight with God in what He has done or is doing. Recognize that His perfect will is better than your own personal will. Strive to do God's will. Many times it may be contrary to what you thought but I promise you by and by you shall see the good in it. For God's thoughts over your life are far greater than your thoughts. So trust God! If you ask the Lord to transform you to be able to see things as He sees them, you will be different from the rest of the other people around you. For you already understand that if God allows anything to come your way, then He knows you can do it and you shall see the good in your life. I promise! Try!

CONCLUSION

People often say that motivation doesn't last. Well, neither does bathing. That's why we recommend it daily.

Zig Ziglar

P raise YE the LORD. Praise, O ye servants of the LORD, praise the name of the LORD.

Blessed be the name of the LORD from this time forth and for evermore.

From the rising of the sun unto going down of same the LORD'S name is to be praised.

The LORD is high above all nations, and his glory above the heavens.

Who is like unto the LORD our God, who dwelleth on high,

Who humbleth himself to behold the things that are in heaven, and in the earth!

He raiseth up the poor out of the dust, and lifteth the needy out of the dunghill;

That he may set him with princes, even with princes of his people.

He maketh the barren woman to keep house, and to be a joyful mother of children. Praise ye the LORD.

Psalms 113

EPILOGUE

When one door of happiness closes, another opens, but often we look so long

at the closed door that we do not see the one that has been opened for us.

Helen Keller

hile I was writing this book, it was refreshing to my spirit as I looked back in my life and saw God's pure love for me. I could identify with God when He was reminding the Israelites the great miracles He did for them from Egypt to Canaan. Many times they forgot the great outstretched powerful hand of God. I always wondered, how could they forget the miracles that God performed like dividing the red sea? I wonder again, why do you forget God when a difficult situation has come your way? So much has happened since then. If the Lord allows me to share the next phase of my journey, it will be my pleasure.

Until then, I wish you all the best in life. When life rocks and pushes you to the corner, just know God promised to never leave nor forsake you. He says all is well; however when we as human beings look at situations we see "bad" happenings and wonder, how come it is contrary to God's promise! It is never contrary . . . just like the musician who quipped, by and by you shall understand it . . . later you see the good and thank God for it. Therefore as a way to living a successful Christian life, you need to recognize that God will never forsake you. Despite the happenings . . . just remember, when Abraham was tempted by God to go and sacrifice Isaac his only loving son. He obeyed because he believed God was able to raise him from death again. Hebrews 19:19 shows that *"Accounting that God was able to raise him up, even from the dead; from whence also he received him in a figure"* (KJV). Interestingly, the Bible used the word, accounting, because Abraham was able to look back and see the things God has done in him and through him all the way from leaving his home country to an unknown land. God was with him all through and blessed him mightily.

The day Jesus was hanged on the cross as a Son of God, he cried and asked; "why have you forsaken me?" God never answered Jesus then, He was silent. This is because Jesus had carried all our sins that when the Father looked at His son, He could not come near him as he was full of sin and filth. He died and was buried, but God's silence never meant He never heard His Son's cry. On the third day at dawn with power and authority, God raised Jesus from the dead. Therefore, he says according to His divine power he has given unto us all things that pertain to life and godliness. The same power that resurrected him from the death is the same power we have through the Holy Spirit. So, my dear reader; understand that God loves you so much and He will do anything for you. You just need to trust and believe him.

Hold on to that promise that surely God will never forsake you! You are His beloved child. He shall bring victory upon our life. Just keep on keeping the faith. He is soon coming for you. For those who do not know Jesus, and do not have an experience with him, just allow Him to show you His love so that you can experience His love. You shall definitely experience God's love over your life. He loves you already. Just accept his love for you. Wow!

Just before I end this book, this is what my husband said:

The Unwritten Chapter
'There is no greater motivation than one's own life'

Whenever you hear your spouse is writing a book, your liver may quiver and shiver for fear that all your dirty linen will be out on display. A can of worms will be opened. When my wife (Tash) told me on phone that she will be writing a book, I was so scared that I volunteered to edit it for her. Your guess is as good as mine. It is not that I am a guru in the English language; I just wasn't sure what was to go out in the public domain especially when she told me it is about her personal life. But one thing I was sure of, my wife has always, even before we met, had a very intimate relationship with God. I remember when we were dating, contrary to popular opinion and belief by then, she would insist on prayer even at odd times. Picture this: in a café bowing and praying before we take a meal! Our children now know that there is no where you cannot pray; she prays with them on phone or on Skype. The other day I saw her laying hands on them on my laptop screen . . . Her journey with God started, as the book depicts, years before we met. Her faith in God has been a constant challenge to me all through our marriage. If faith was measurable, I almost wouldn't meet her standards. I am more of 'by actions' while she is more of 'by faith' (talk of complementing each other). Her education basically has been a matter of faith from financial provision to opportunities to advance. For any reader who may assume that it has all been rosy, please make a date with me. They say that without pain, there would be no gain.

As a family we missed her so much especially during the many foreign trips, studies and the many late night classes. I had to multitask and fill in for her during those times. We have had our share of struggles from lack of finances, illnesses, death of close friends and family members, struggles with in-laws and not to mention the times we would have wished to attend social functions together. As couples, I always say that when you say 'I do' you really have to be ready because the verb 'do' includes so much that pastors never tabulate for us. The journey just begins then. When we got married, I realized that she had an internal desire to pursue her career. I promised to walk with her every single step. Hadn't I said 'I do'? We have faithfully albeit painfully walked the journey and as I await her doctorate graduation, I can only say that God has fulfilled her heart's desire and made me an instrument in the fulfilment of His promise. Tash has challenged me so much in writing that I promise to write and tell you the reader what was happening behind the scenes. Case in point: in our busy schedules of balancing between work and class, we more often than not forgot our roles as husband and wife that we almost became classmates in the house. That is a story for another day.

Tash, your life is a testimony that we have a faithful God who is interested in us beyond measure. For anyone out there, married or otherwise, and you have a dream that is not yet achieved, this is your time, wake up and go for it. The rest will follow. But remember, seek first the Kingdom of God, and all else will be added to you (I think there is such a verse in the bible.)

Written by Willie Mwangi—that loving and caring husband who was mentioned somewhere in this book.

ABOUT THE AUTHOR

Dorothy Muthoka—Kagwaini is an Accounting lecturer, with ten years of working experience as well as five years of teaching experience. She is currently pursuing her PhD in the same field. Dorothy, always shares her life's journey as a way of building lasting relationships. She has a contagious smile.

REFERENCES

Jakes, T. D. (April, 2013). _Your Answer Blows in the Wind._ Retrieved from: www.tdjakes.org. Dated 30th April 2013.

Holy Bible King James referring BibleZondervan Publishers, Grand Rapids, Michigan. 2000.

Mwangi, W. (2010). _Determined to Succeed_. Output Magazine. Daystar University Publishers.

Muthoka, M. Dorothy. (2010). _Women in the Hall_. An Article Published by Council for Christian Colleges and Universities.

Peterson, H. Eugene. (1997) *Leap over a Wall: Earthly Spiritually for Everyday Christians*. Harper Collins Publisher. New York.

Prince, Joseph. (October, 2013). *Receive your Victory*. Retrieved from www.jesephprince.org. Dated 19th October, 2013.